20,-
FP
#62093

An Urgent Request
Sarah Luczaj

An Urgent Request

Fortunate Daughter is an imprint of Tebot Bach.

Editor: Cecilia Woloch.

Design, Layout: Caron Andregg

Cover Design: Agnieszka Stańczak

ISBN: 978-1-893670-36-5

Library of Congress Control Number: 2009926107

A Tebot Bach book

The Fortunate Daughter Mission is to publish, annually, one chapbook by an exceptional poet who has not yet published a chapbook or book.

Tebot Bach, Welsh for little teapot, is a non-profit public benefit corporation which sponsors workshops, forums, lectures and publications. Tebot Bach books are distributed by Small Press Distribution, Armadillo, and Ingram.

The Tebot Bach Mission: Advancing literacy, strengthening community, and transforming life experiences with the power of poetry through readings, workshops, and publications.

www.tebotbach.org

CONTENTS

FOR JOSÉ DROUET
(1968 –1989)

José, the light is moving in the water
José I carved a poem in the walls of a room

the room was dust
and the planets were
trapped as the people
in it and it broke
on them, and the room
broke on the sky which
is made of dirt as
the room is made of
dirt and the people
are made of dirt
and also the stars

it broke
on your body made of stars
José and now the words
are set in those walls
forever, too deep, and no one
is allowed to stand
between them, my room
sits alone in the city
José the light is moving in the water
and you are a mouthful
a handful now, a scattering

I wanted to tell you this
José who broke the windows

José the room was dust

THE NOISE IS STILL THERE

However hard I swallow, however tightly I clench my fists, however loudly I sing, and whatever silence I move into my heart. While I spin from head to belly and the water rises and however calm it is. Whether I am aware of my breathing or drunk, if I practice the violin or not, and particularly when opening doors. When I lie down with my man and child, full of love, without thinking, or even feeling, 'mine'. When weeding flowerbeds, when I feel I belong, when I know that for some absurd reason, the walls are exactly that shade of yellow, the sun is shining straight down on us yet again and in my life at this small moment, everything is fine. When I have said everything and feel complete. Even and especially then.

OH MY GIRL

knocking on the door with cold hands, saying you
couldn't sleep
my girl, with the longest umbilical cord, bloody and
stretched from dancing
my girl, with a too heavy rucksack, waving at me from
the future
sucking my breasts in the past

oh my girl, wanting to be somewhere and someone else
to be fat, to be thin, to be loved, to be left, to leave
oh my girl with a bag full of tears
and a star in her step

oh my girl with the endless water
looking for a bank to knock against
looking for a boat to carry
oh my girl, wondering what's wrong with you that the
world isn't right

my girl, lying on your back in the fallen leaves next to me
the last of the sunlight on your face
my girl frightened to say and not to say
oh my girl triumphant in the snow

oh my girl asleep next to me
breathing on my face, your mind a mystery
oh my girl, your laughter spills and falls and pools like
water
my girl with sharp glass in her hands

oh my girl, wanting to fill yourself and empty yourself
oh my girl, trying and trying, feeding your babies and
wanting to scream
oh my girl, buying another pair of pink shoes
oh my girl, the D string, the one long note of you.

ORANGE

I wake two heart-inches from the wall.
To die is to learn to live
on air, you wrote in poems,
in overdose writing, schoolgirl
characters, on a tablecloth hemmed
with flowers that each were your name.

Goodbye forever, you wrote, signing
my dream where you should.
You can't see me and I take
my face from the wall.
I go to the window.
I put it into rain.

MY LIFE IS BRILLIANT

No one I love
has died so far today

every single war in this world
has passed me by

I am not starving and I haven't stumbled
onto any terrorist's map
or into anyone's axis of evil

nobody tortured me today
no policeman shot me by accident or on purpose
no tidal wave swept my house away

I was not sentenced to death for infidelity
blasphemy, murder
or not having put enough salt in the soup

BACK

I walk out of the graveyard
imagining the treetops
waking up so far from earth unable
to come down. I walk
away from you, towards you, feeling space
between the arch of each foot and the ground.

I want to live
on cherry blossoms and fistfuls of snow—
walking away
from you, towards you, towards the cars
scraping the air black with noise
the sun in the grass.

HERE IS A LIST OF THINGS I ATE YESTERDAY...

she says:

Fifty pounds—eaten
ten sandwiches
five packets of crisps
ten bars of chocolate
and all of my clothes

First stirrings of fear—eaten
tremblings of wonder—eaten
a lot of bad music, and the television
I ate my own bed
I ate the full moon

For one blank moment
on the floor of the toilet cubicle
the whole damned world was eaten

All the dirt—eaten
he didn't see me—he was eaten
all my worthlessness—eaten
I lay curled up
on the toilet floor—eaten

Then I retched it all up
I came back
one, blissful moment

And then I started
to eat the world
again

WASHING HER

She wriggles up towards me like a worm
swollen, rained on. Feels
the water's thud, opens
and shuts her lips, hears
little noises escape,
standing, swaying, suddenly forgetting
half-way through a movement what it was—

stopping the slow dance. Something's left stranded
into atoms, the rain. It joins
the dark matter of
the universe, invisible
loves, against which
life holds us fast. She's sensing
her exact distance from the surface. 'I can't
move', she says, and moves.

MISSING THE DEAD

If I could catch some daylight
as I catch
the snow melting from the roof
I could bring a bucketful
inside
and pour it out until it fills the room
in the middle of the night.

AN URGENT REQUEST

Hello and goodbye,
flour, vegetables, coffee
and orange juice.
A body, a soul, thoughts,
a moment of freedom.
Words I am so jealous of your words.

I would like to buy some Polish grammar.
All of it.

I would like to buy a reusable bag
for the case endings.
Please segregate the genitive
from the dative well.

If war were to break out tomorrow
which of the neighbours would kill us?
How do they all know what to do?
How do my friends walk around
with all they know and feel?
Why won't they talk to each other?

It's just a question of words—
the wrong ones got delivered.
They don't fit.

We fear our words say
something about us
instead of using those damned words to speak.

We gravitate irresistibly
towards the passive.
Mostly women.

I am furious.

Deliver those words please,
I cannot wait any longer.

I need not only the perfect
and imperfect verbs
and each separate verb-concept
but a precise dividing line
between them.

I know that will be more expensive.

I am prepared to pay postage.

Yes, the country I live in
really exists.

It is called where-I-am-now
or, for short, my name.
It's even in Europe.
So, you see, it won't cost so much.
This document will most certainly
even be translated.

I know exactly where I am.
You understand?
First you have to give me the words!

I'm leaning over the desk now
and my hair is falling over the forms
and I'm sweating.

Yes, I need prepositions too.
And the cases to which they attach.

I need those little joining wires.
Several thousand of them.

They'll be cheaper if I buy them
all at once.

I don't need poetry.
I already have a body.

Just give me the words.

THAW

if your silence should fall
from balance, from form,
from branches to water
with a sliding sound
from the green leaves
left behind,
I would catch it
with my mouth
and ask you to touch
with your tongue the snow inside.

HOW TO TAKE CONTROL OF YOUR OWN LIFE

Only enter churches
after dark.
Walk with muddy shoes.
Cut with the knife pointing

Away from you.
Laugh loudly. Walk on the grass.

Remember that one train
may hide another. Always
brush your teeth. Don't
listen to advice.

Recycle advice.
Turn advice inside out.

Keep a hold on your soul.
Store this product
in a cool, dark, dry place.
Keep it away from naked flames.

Carelessness causes fires.
Walk through fires.

Be careless. Always
wear clean underwear
in case you get run over.
Listen, don't listen.

Don't wear underwear.
Don't get run over.

POST SCRIPT

it should never have happened—OK.
now at what point exactly should it have stopped
  happening?

should the sky that night have stopped its impractical
  translucence?
should you have stopped sitting opposite me, then
  stopped sitting next to me—

could you have stopped your eyes from flashing?
should you have done up the top button on your shirt

before you left your house? should I have worn different
  socks?
as we walked across the grass to the lit room

wrapped in blankets could we have just stopped?
should we have gone back to the afternoon then

said goodbye not hello in the morning?

IMPERATIVE

The bare infinitive
is used to issue orders

Take off your glasses
('50% of your intelligence')
Take off that awful grey sweater
And all the green and blue ones too

Take off religion
Take off your headache
That's good, now, closer
Now take off your voice
Leave your eyes, for now

And I'll take off my arguments
'Relativism'
My skirt
Coffee, and bells
Your confession

I'll take off words

That's good now, closer
Now I'm taking off desire

Watch me

RE: MORE SPILLING

thanks for your letter
I send you in return

a fire
and a waterfall

BLAZE

It's autumn, season of mooching poets, mellow
fruitfulness and death, of blazing lanterns
standing in the trees, of crunching dry gold

standing, of black skeletons poking through,
of apples, I want to straighten my spine,
eat gold leaves, rocket down

to earth scuttle across someone's face, someone
lying naked in a field, sun bleeding through eyelids
thinking last time, defiant joy, I want to be it

and the wind that breaks up the block of blue
that fits over us today, the wind that makes
its sea sound in my hair, the wind that rushes

over the flat stones at the door, the stones
from the riverbed, the wind that grasps
the leaves and flings them high and brightness

HOLIDAY

Sitting among huge white caravans
where French and Dutch couples, just
tipped over the edge of middle age, polished
their doorsteps under the palm trees,
it seemed that it couldn't get worse.

Where to go, to find peace?
Get the night train over the High Atlas
and leave for the sea in the morning?
But that's a city, by the sea, still a city
and we always argue by the sea.

Stay here? In the hotel like a hospital?
That's exactly what I need! I hate holidays.
I could spend my money much better at home.
Home, what home? I feel better here!
Our daughter would like to go to the sea.

The baby eats dirt. Wandering tearstained
and hopeless, we stumble across—
a swimming pool!
The blue eye of God, the answer
right in front of our noses!

And yes, they have rooms here!
Ecstatic, exulted, we make our way
back to the hotel for our towels.
We get picked up by a donkey trailer
on the way. Ten dirhams.

Children shriek with laughter
as I sway, ungainly, on the plank,
baby on my back, and a young man on a bicycle
rides alongside, asks us how many
languages we know.

We pack in a flash and start the long, dusty walk
back. We decide to time ourselves, I use
my grandmother's watch. The sun beats down.
Half an hour. We arrive, change, my daughter sits
waiting for me to test the water.

I look down and—
I can't do it.
I sit there some more,
run it every way in my head
and I still can't do it.

I have to do it, for my daughter.
I have to and I can't.
The bright blue swimming pool
gazes at me, deadly, with its unchlorinated eye.
I turn, grab my top, and something flies

through the air
to land at the bottom
of the pool with what would be
a sickening thud
if it made any noise at all.

The object
now lying at the bottom of the devil's bright eye—
is my grandmother's watch.
Lying like a dead animal, lying like an object
in a swimming pool in the south of Morocco.

"It's unchlorinated" says the Frenchman at the table.
"It's dangerous. Don't go in. Are you French? No?
    English? Well,
we all have our problems. *How* did you travel? By
Moroccan bus?" I'm crying now. My grandmother's watch
if it could, would wink at me.

It lies there, like irretrievable loss
within arm's reach.
My husband tries.
"This isn't
a swimming pool!" he cries,

"It's a trap! It's specially designed
to drown people! There's no way in!
There's no way out!" He gets out, disgusted
with those who have things, those who lose things,
and those who want to swim.

"Everywhere we go!" he fumes, "you lose
your grandmother's watch!"
I wipe my tears and mutter that
I just want that Frenchman to go away.
I ask a girl for help, who fetches her brother

who fetches a long iron pole, bent at the end
just perfect for fishing out
grandmothers' watches.
Up, up it comes, as on a rusty crane
then flies back down again—

we groan *ensemble*
like the crowd at a firework display
in reverse.
And finally, up, up it rises and lands,
safe, showing the last hour,

completely useless. *Never mind*, we say.
We know that nothing is going to work now.
There's a strange, glorious, exhausted
sense of relief.
We open its back and lay it in the sun.

WHAT MORE CAN I ASK FOR

these days I like to sleep
with my arms above my head
fingers entwined
feet clasped
big toes interlocked

breasts filling and bubbling
belly rounding and ripening
full of eyes, hands
and the wash of emotion before thought

my body stretched out like a boomerang
or a paper plane
ready to be thrown
ready

to fly across the room
and hit the wall
or slice through the window and into the sky

CHILD SONG

Wood warp, feather, fish scale, skin
I carry their print inside my eyes
The world is stamped, the world goes in

Some of these patterns are called a sin
But I don't kneel, and I don't rise
Wood warp, feather, fish scale, skin

For if you do, you still can't win
The priest will cut you down to size
The world is stamped, the world goes in

And I am silent, watchful, thin
I smile and grown-ups think I'm wise
Wood warp, feather, fish scale, skin

I keep my secrets in a tin
I keep my smile as my disguise
The world is stamped, the world goes in

I was born a clear, empty thing
I had no hope, and told no lies
Wood warp, feather, fish scale, skin
The world is stamped, the world goes in.

BARKING BACK

I'd tell anyone with depression: don't believe the
thoughts in your mind. Don't walk the black dog.
Walk where there are people— G.P. Taylor

Don't do it, they say. Don't walk
the black dog.
Don't look it in the eyes.

I watched it long enough. I watched it
until it curled up and slept.

No more. I'm opening my eyes
wide enough to cause accidents. I'm blowing
the whistle, and letting go
of the lead. I'm eating the distance. Oh my
god, I'm breathing. I'm getting up
now with my palms open

and my boots on.

THE SOUP NEEDS ATTENTION

and here I am, in the sea.

Seeking solitude
seeking screens, seeking
shade, seeking
freedom of movement
which does not begin with 's'
although sex does.

When I tilt my head back
in the water
all the cries I hear combined say
'Mama!'

A little more, and I hear
the water coiling
small necklaces in my ears.

I can see sky, a white cloud.
I ask it—do you need
attention? It doesn't. I ask
the sea, it doesn't. I ask
myself, she says

no, no, let's swim a little further.

ACKNOWLEDGMENTS

Some of these poems have appeared in the following publications:

yefief: "Washing Her" and "For Jose Drouet"
Cider Press Review: "Thaw" and 'what more can i ask for'
Clarion Review: "Cover"
LA Review: "Imperative" (under the title "The Strip Poem")
Natural Bridge: "Child Song"
www.thepedestalmagazine.com: "An Urgent Request"

"Missing the Dead," "Thaw," "How to Take Control Of Your Own Life", and "Washing Her" all appear in the collection *This Line on The Map* containing English and Polish versions of poems with co-authors Wacław Turek and Cecilia Woloch, published by Krośnieńska Oficyna Wydawnicza (the Krosno Publishing House) in Poland.

"oh my girl," "The Noise Is Still There," and "The Soup Needs Attention" appear in the anthology *oh my girl*, which collects the work of Vesna Denčić, Christine Herzer, Olga Lalić Krowicka, Slavenka Lalić and Sarah Luczaj in English, Polish and Serbian, soon to be published in Serbia. A chapbook version of the anthology is online at *www.languageandculture.net*.

Several of the poems have appeared in Polish, Croatian and Serbian print and online journals and anthologies. "Washing her" has been danced by the *Strecz* contemporary dance group in Krosno, Poland.

Sarah Luczaj is a British poet, translator and psychotherapist living (with her husband and two daughters) and working in rural Poland since 1997. She has translated, and published widely, the poems of Polish poet Halina Poświatowska and the poetry collection "Songs of a Dead Rooster" by Ukrainian writer Yuri Andrukhovych. Presently writing a PhD on Buddhism and psychotherapy, she runs an online therapy practice at www.mytherapist.com.